D1370702

MYSELF

Written by
Rhonda Reeves

Illustrated by
Cheryl Totty

Missions and Me Series
Woman's Missionary Union
Birmingham, AL 35283-0010

Published by Woman's Missionary Union, SBC
P.O. Box 830010
Birmingham, AL 35283-0010

© 2001 by Woman's Missionary Union, SBC
All rights reserved. First printing 2001
Printed in China
Woman's Missionary Union® and WMU® are registered trademarks.

Dewey Decimal Classification: CE
Subject Headings: God (Christianity)

Series: Missions and Me
ISBN: 1-56309-360-X
W018101•0601•5M

Look at me. I am wonderfully made.

God made me,
and I am His.

God is good to me.

God gave me ears to hear my dog, Timber, when he barks at the neighbor's cat.

God gave me eyes to see all the beautiful
colors of the world—red, blue,
yellow, purple, and green!

God gave me a nose to smell the roses
in my grandmother's garden. He gave me
a mouth so I could taste the good food
He gives me, and say thank You, God,
for good things to enjoy.

God gave me arms and legs so I could run
and play in the park with my friends.

God loves me so much and
helps me to love others.

Every day I am learning to be
more like Jesus.

I help others.

I pray for others.

The Bible tells me God cares about me.

The Bible tells me God will love me always.

I will be glad
and sings songs
to God. I will
give thanks to
God for He is
good to me.